This Composition Notebook

BELONGS TO:

CONTENT

Page	Subject

CONTENT

Page	Subject

CONTENT

Page	Subject

CONTENT

Page	Subject

Made in the USA
Monee, IL
01 September 2022

13073274R00070